Havanese
20 Milestone Challenges

Havanese Memorable Moments. Includes Milestones for Memories, Gifts, Grooming, Socialization & Training

Volume 2

Todays Doggy

Dedicated To All of You Wonderful Owners and Fans

Introduction

Welcome to the Original Doggy Milestone Series™ where you are encouraged to create those special moments with your dog. We have composed the milestones in a way that challenges you to set the stage before taking your photos.

Use props and make it fun - be creative in setting up your photos. Get family and friends involved - take it out with you - use it in different places and settings - have a play with it and most importantly, have a good time!

You can either hold the desired milestone spread open yourself - or have somebody hold it open as you take the snap.

If you would like to have the selected milestone book spread open and standing independently in your photos, you can use one or two large 'foldback' clips to hold the spread open.

Share your photos with friends, family, and communities - look for feedback and areas of improvements in order to create even better memorable photos.

Good luck and enjoy your photo fun.

I
Noticed
You
Were
Sleeping...

So I Helped You Finish The Food

I Look
Rather
Fetching

...Don't
I?

I've
Got a
Million
Dollar
Idea

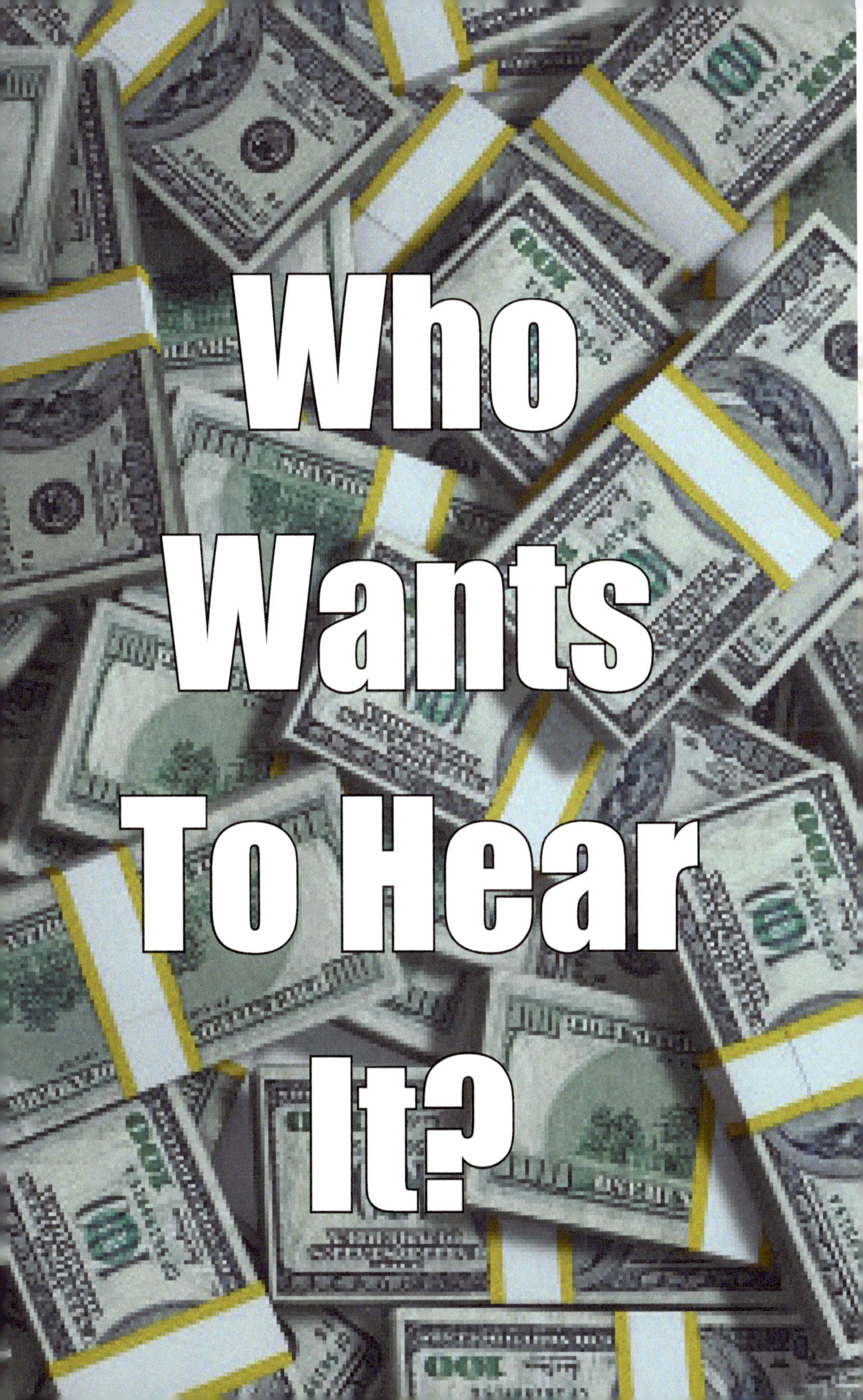
Who
Wants
To Hear
It?

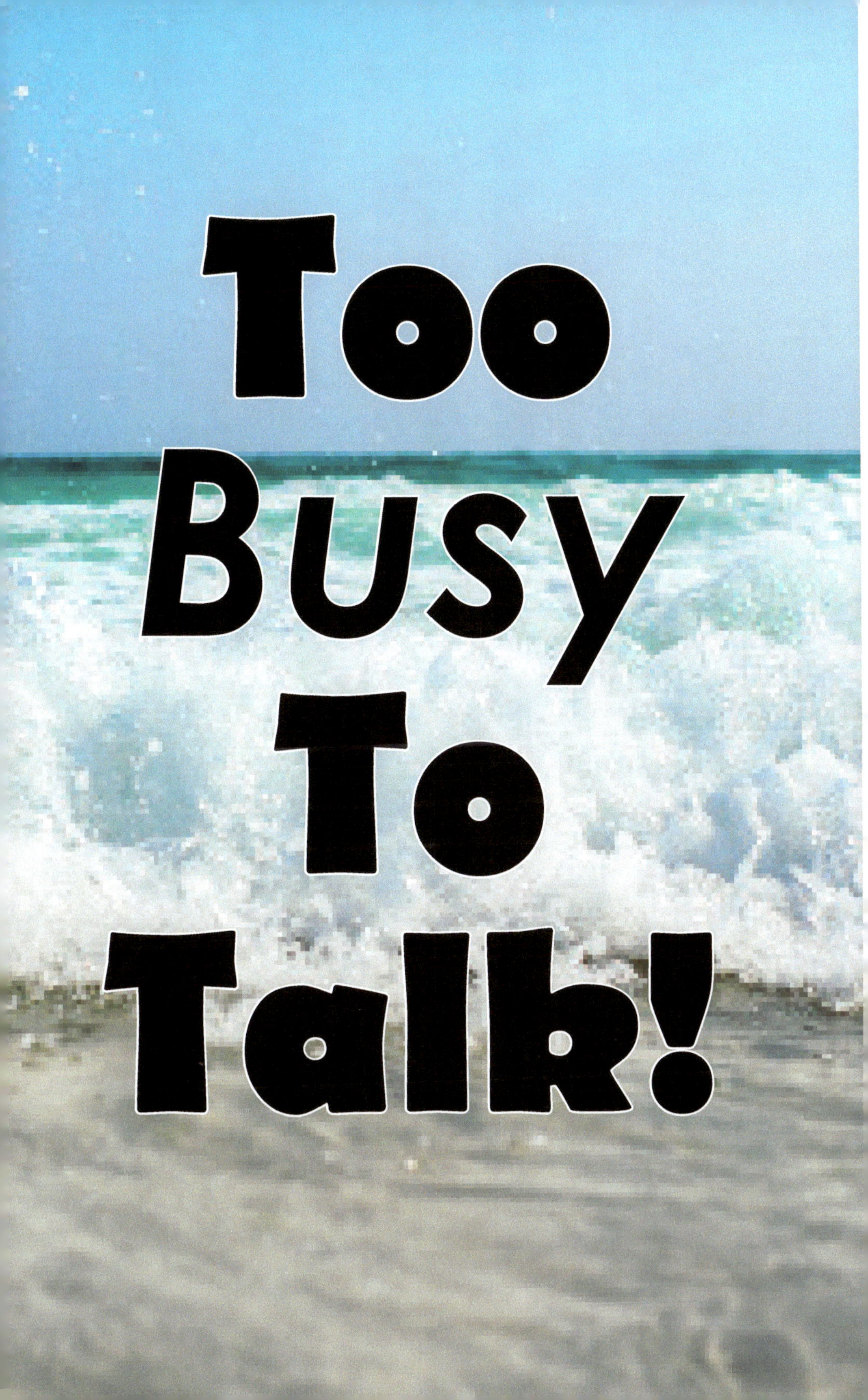
Too
Busy
To
Talk!

I'M BBBAD

...Bad To The Bone

Today...

Was a "RUFF!" Day

I Have No Idea

What I'm Doing

WHEN YOU'RE HOME ALONE

AND SOMEONE KNOCKS ON THE DOOR...

MIRROR MIRROR ON THE WALL...

Who's The **Doggiest** Of Them All?

I'm So GREAT

I Even Know How To High 5

Ahh...

The Joys of Being Groomed

Oh Hey!

You're Home Early!

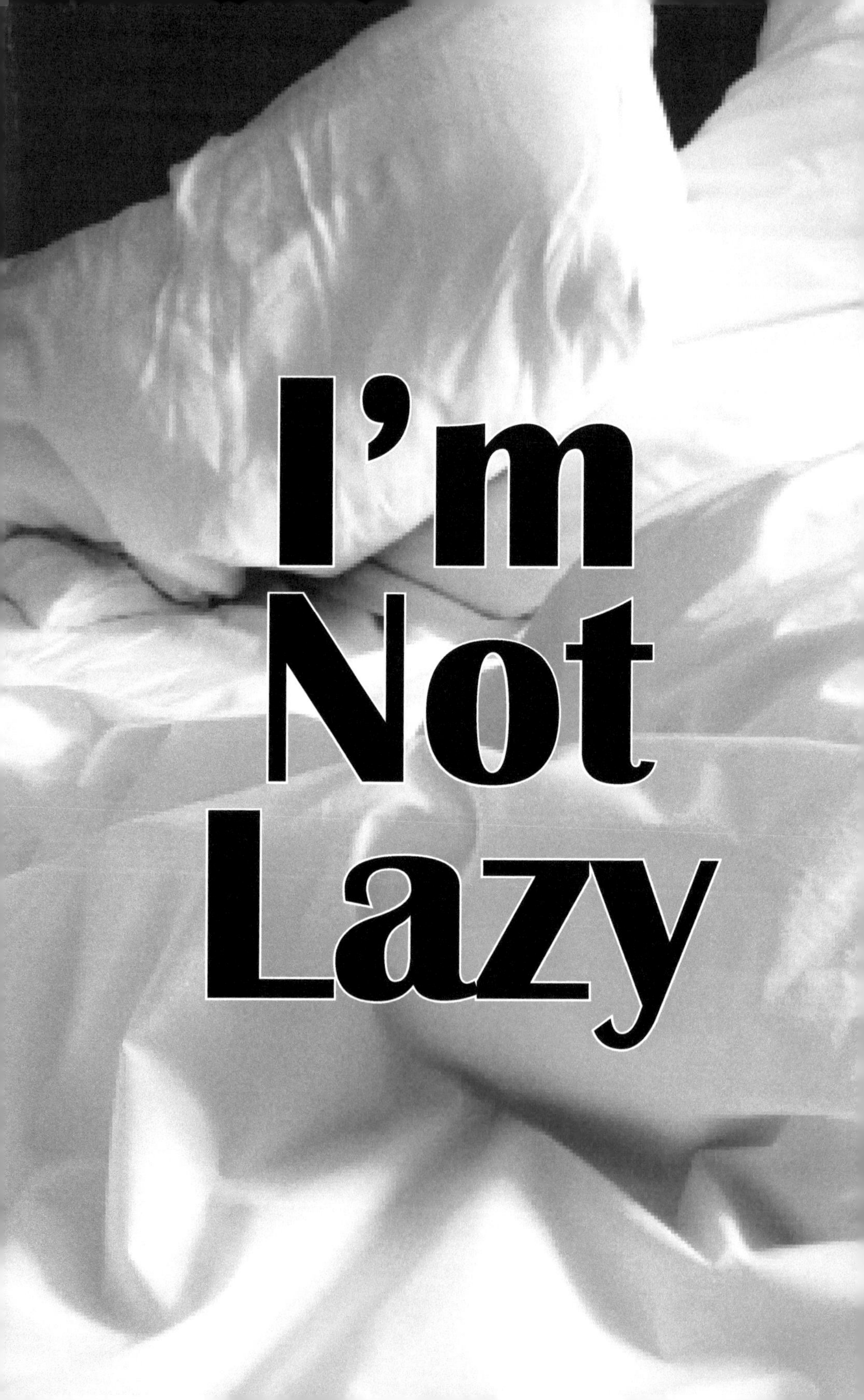
I’m
Not
Lazy

I'm Just On Energy Saving Mode

OH LOOK!

Someone Has Made a Mess!

I Wonder Who Did It!?

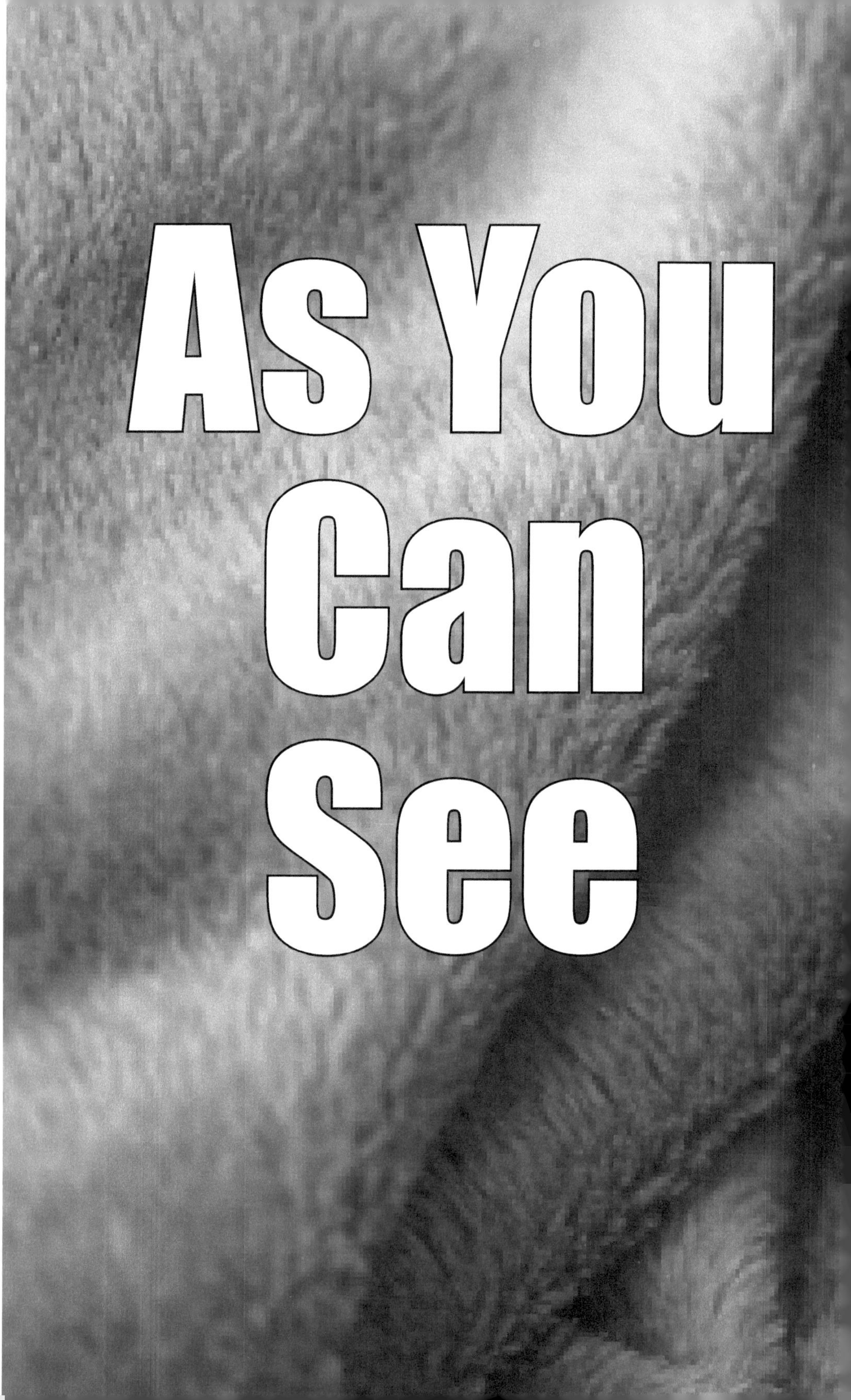
As You
Can
See

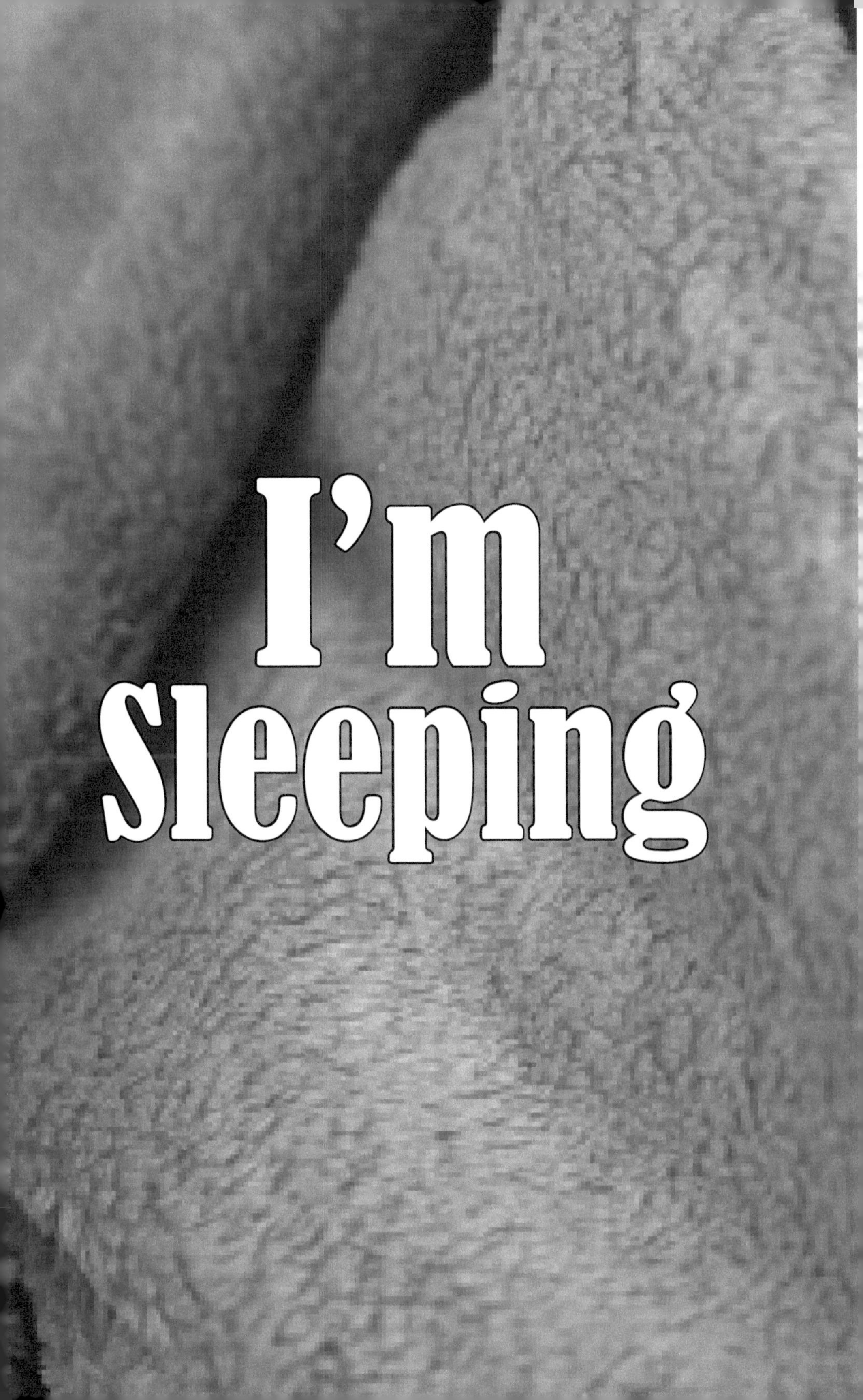
I’m
Sleeping

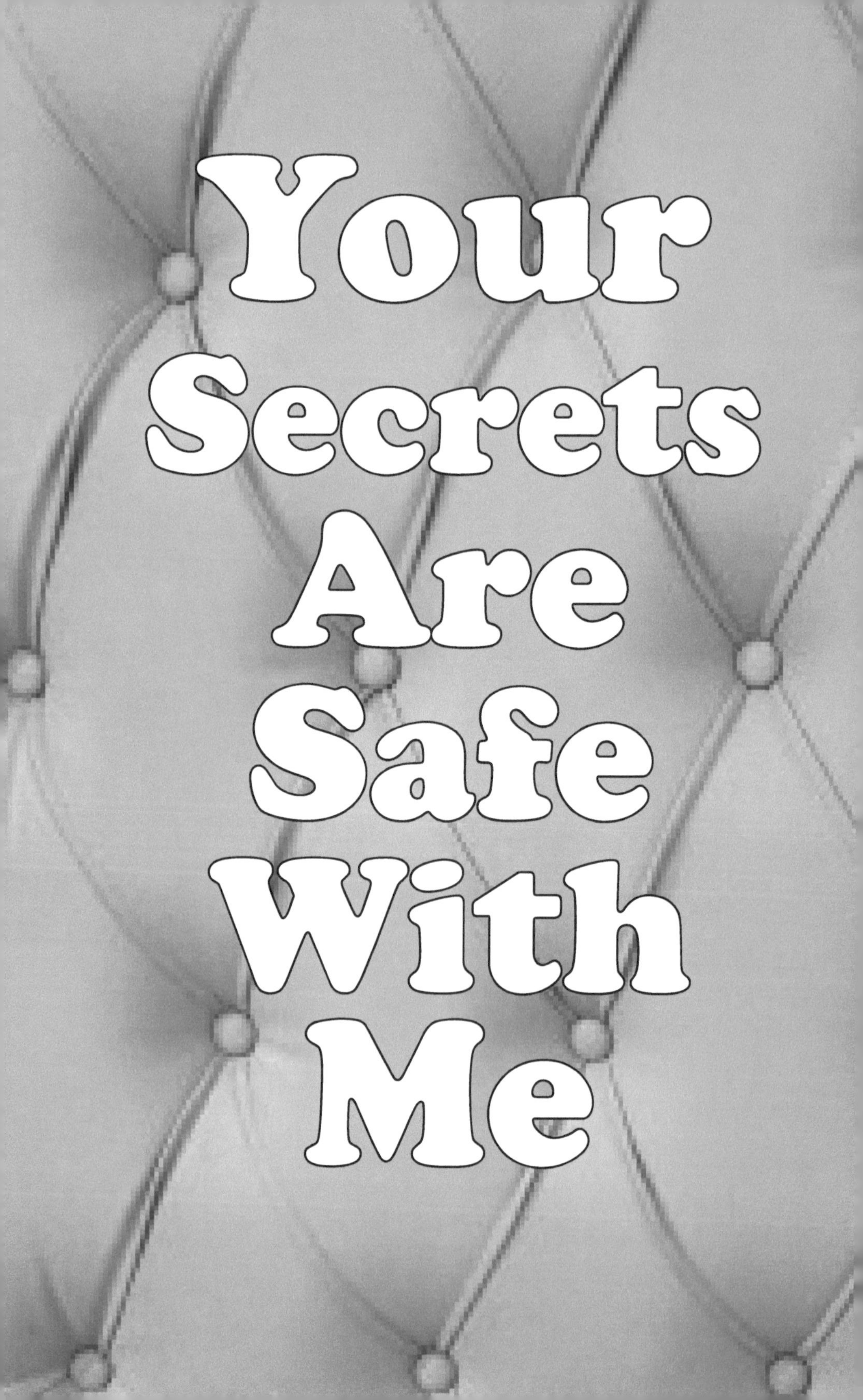
Your Secrets Are Safe With Me

I'm Always Listening

CHEEE

EEESE

My Dog's Reaction When I Say...

I
LOVE
YOU

I’m Ready

For My Bedtime Story

I've Got It All...

Under Control

www.ingramcontent.com/pod-product-compliance
Lightning Source LLC
Chambersburg PA
CBHW041510010526
44118CB00006B/211
9781395864088